CÉSAR CHÁVEZ

By Jonatha A. Brown

WORLD ALMANAC® LIBRARY

Please visit our web site at: www.worldalmanaclibrary.com
For a free color catalog describing World Almanac® Library's list
of high-quality books and multimedia programs, call 1-800-848-2928 (USA)
or 1-800-387-3178 (Canada). World Almanac® Library's fax: (414) 332-3567.

Library of Congress Cataloging-in-Publication Data

Brown, Jonatha A.
    César Chávez / by Jonatha A. Brown.
      p. cm. — (Trailblazers of the modern world)
    Includes bibliographical references and index.
    Summary: Traces the life and accomplishments of Mexican American labor leader César Chávez,
who founded the United Farm Workers union to promote better wages and working conditions for
migrants and other farm workers.
    ISBN 0-8368-5097-1 (lib. bdg.)
    ISBN 0-8368-5257-5 (softcover)
    1. Chávez, César, 1927-1993—Juvenile literature. 2. Migrant agricultural laborers—Labor unions—
United States—Officials and employees—Biography—Juvenile literature. 3. Mexican Americans—
Biography—Juvenile literature. [1. Chávez, César, 1927-1993. 2. Labor leaders. 3. Migrant labor.
4. United Farm Workers. 5. Mexican Americans—Biography.] I. Title. II. Series.
HD6509.C48B76   2004
331.88'13'092—dc22
[B]   2003058743

First published in 2004 by
World Almanac® Library
330 West Olive Street, Suite 100
Milwaukee, WI 53212 USA

Copyright © 2004 by World Almanac® Library.

Project manager: Jonny Brown
Editor: Jim Mezzanotte
Design and page production: Scott M. Krall
Photo research: Diane Laska-Swanke
Indexer: Walter Kronenberg

Photo credits: © AP/Wide World Photos: 43 bottom; © Bettmann/CORBIS: 7, 18, 29, 41, 42; © CORBIS: 5, 8, 10, 15;
© Farrell Grehan/CORBIS: 27; © Hulton Archive/Getty Images: cover, 9, 11, 16, 39; © Mike Nelson/AFP/Getty
Images: 43 top; © Michael Rougier/Time Life Pictures/Getty Images: 12, 14, 20, 21, 36; © Michael Salas/Time Life
Pictures/Getty Images: 25; © Arthur Schatz/Time Life Pictures/Getty Images: 24; © Flip Schulke/CORBIS: 28
bottom; © Ted Streshinsky/CORBIS: 22, 23, 30; Walter Reuther Library, Wayne State University: 4, 13, 17, 19, 28
top, 31, 32, 33, 34, 37

Printed in the United States of America

1 2 3 4 5 6 7 8 9 08 07 06 05 04

TENTS

Words that appear in the glossary are printed in **boldface**
type the first time they occur in the text.

CHAPTER 1

FIELD WORKER'S HERO

César Chávez was an unlikely leader. Short, soft-spoken, and very shy, this Mexican-American farm worker was someone you could easily overlook in a crowd. Even the possibility of personal success seemed remote. After all, he had no schooling beyond the eighth grade, no money, and certainly no connections in influential business and political circles. He did not even speak English as a first language.

César Chávez led farm workers in California in a nonviolent fight for their rights and dignity.

Despite those disadvantages, in the 1960s César Chávez **organized** and led the first successful agricultural **labor union** in the continental United States. Through that union, he helped millions of desperately poor people improve their lives. He worked on behalf of the *campesinos*, the field workers who pick the fruits and vegetables sold in supermarkets everywhere. Together, he and the poor, largely illiterate campesinos demanded and finally received fairer treatment from many powerful farmers and corporate giants who had been taking advantage of farm workers for decades. Their efforts eventually led to changes in the laws that govern farm labor. Under César's leadership, the campesinos improved their own lives and the lives of generations of farm workers to come.

WORKING IN THE FIELDS

Tending and harvesting fruits and vegetables is demanding, uncomfortable work. Men, women, and children spend days and weeks at a time working in awkward positions as they pick low-growing crops, such as strawberries, or those that grow above their heads, such as apples. Sometimes the only chance the workers have to stand up straight comes when they haul crates of produce to huge trucks parked at the edge of the fields.

For many years, uncomfortable positions and hard work were the least of the campesinos' problems. Before 1967, laws that set a minimum wage for most workers did not apply to farm labor. As a result, farmers could pay their hired help much less than the minimum wage, and some farm workers took home only pennies a day. There were also no laws covering basic sanitation and health standards for field work. Thousands of laborers worked outdoors all day without bathrooms, shade, or a source of drinking water. Many were routinely exposed

Harvesting lettuce means working bent over for hours at a time. It is hardly surprising that many field workers develop severe back problems.

to pesticides and other chemicals that made them sick. To make matters worse, they could not get health or unemployment insurance, so any injury or illness might mean starvation for them and their families.

If the campesinos had been in the mainstream of American life, they probably would not have tolerated these inhumane working conditions. If they had been in the mainstream, most would have found other work or at least complained to representatives in Congress about the unfair labor laws. But after World War II (1939–1945), most field workers were unskilled laborers from terribly poor parts of Mexico, other Latin American countries, and Asia. Very few understood, read, or spoke English. Most could not ask simple questions of their employers, much less complain to representatives in Congress. Worse yet, they could not read English-language newspapers, understand U.S. news broadcasts, or otherwise learn about and participate in life in the United States. Isolated and poorly informed, the campesinos were easy prey for bosses who wanted to profit from their ignorance.

A LEADER EMERGES

César Chávez became a field worker when he was just a boy. He, his brothers and sisters, and their parents worked in the fields up and down the West Coast of the United States for many years. Sometimes the pay was so bad that, at the end of the day, the whole family had earned little more than a dollar. Unable to afford decent housing, they slept under bridges, in old cars, and in dilapidated shacks or tents that had no water or electricity. To put a little food on the table, César and his siblings often foraged for wild greens and fished in irrigation canals. Many times, the family was almost starving.

A 1960 survey of farm workers in Fresno County, California, showed that 25 percent had no refrigeration, 25 percent had no flush toilets, and less than 50 percent had running water in their homes. When this migrant family was photographed in 1958, their travels had taken them to Virginia.

César believed that no human being deserved to live in such poverty and despair. The tough question, however, was this: what could he or anyone do to change the situation? He knew that most field workers did not vote, so elected officials were not likely to pay attention to them. And he understood that charity might provide temporary support, but it could not truly solve the problem. Eventually, Chávez became convinced that the campesinos had only one hope for improving their lives: they had to band together in a labor union and demand fair treatment from their employers.

Since he thought of this effort as a fight for human dignity, César Chávez was committed to treating others respectfully. He believed that if, and only if, the campesinos worked together and behaved reasonably and responsibly—without violence—they could regain their self-respect and force growers to treat them fairly. Supported by little more than this passionate belief in the power of **nonviolent confrontation**, César Chávez began his life's work.

CHAPTER 2

CHILDHOOD

César Chávez's grandparents came to the United States from Mexico in the late 1800s. Settling in North Gila Valley, Arizona, they bought land, built a sturdy adobe house, and worked on their ranch for nearly fifty years.

One of their children was a boy named Librado. He grew up in North Gila Valley and eventually married another Mexican immigrant, Juana Estrada. Together they worked on the ranch, ran three small businesses—a store, a garage, and a pool hall—and had children.

Farming was hard, sweaty work when César was a boy—especially for farmers who could not afford tractors.

RANCH LIFE

César Estrada Chávez, the second of Librado and Juana's children, was born on March 31, 1927. He was a shy little boy who was uncomfortable with strangers and preferred the security of his close-knit, Spanish-speaking family. And what a large family he had—five brothers and sisters, as well as parents, grandparents, many aunts and uncles, and dozens of cousins.

Although the family was close, the children sometimes argued and fought. When that happened, Juana Chávez reminded them that violence was no way to solve problems. According to César, "She would always talk to us about not fighting, not responding in kind. She taught her children to reject that part of a culture which too often tells its young men that you're not a man if you don't fight back. She would say, 'It's best to turn the other cheek. God gave you senses, like your eyes and mind and tongue, so that you can get out of anything.'"

When César was young, all of the Chávez children had to help around the house, in Librado's businesses, and on their grandparents' ranch. According to César's older sister Rita, César was usually the one who organized everyone's chores: "[He] would tell us, you feed those two horses and I'll feed this cow; he always had everybody assigned to something." After finishing their chores, the children could always find something interesting to do—ride horses, swim, hike, play at the pool hall, or wait on customers at the family store.

While César was growing up in Arizona, the Great Depression was taking a heavy toll on people all over the United States and the world. Millions were out of work and could not pay their bills. In North Gila Valley, more and more of Librado's customers could not pay for their purchases. César's father eventually had to sell all of his businesses because he had so few paying customers. Fortunately, the Chávez family still had the ranch, and as long as they had those 160 acres (65 hectares), they could grow their own food and manage to get by.

During the Great Depression, many people roamed from town to town looking for work.

In 1933, a severe drought hit Arizona and much of the West. Without water, Librado's crops died, and he fell behind in paying property taxes. After four years of drought and failed crops, the government **confiscated** the family's ranch for nonpayment of taxes. It was a terrible blow. César later remembered, "My mother came

The Great Depression

The 1930s were difficult for people everywhere. Serious problems started in 1929 when stock prices fell drastically on the New York Stock Exchange. Tens of thousands of people who had invested in the stock market lost almost all their money. Over the next few years, these people bought fewer goods and services. And because businesses had fewer customers, many banks, factories, and other businesses had to trim their staffs or close down completely. By 1932, between twelve and fifteen million people were out of work in the United States and hundreds of thousands had lost their homes. Many homeless, jobless people roamed aimlessly from town to town. These people, often called hobos, were highly visible examples of the desperate circumstances into which so many had fallen.

When César's family became migrant, they joined hordes of other homeless people, like these, who lived in tents, trucks, and other makeshift shelters.

out of the house crying, we children knew there was trouble. . . . And we had to leave." He went on to say, "We left everything behind. Left chickens and cows and horses and all the implements. Things belonging to my father's family and my mother's as well. Everything." Landowners no longer, the Chávezes were homeless and nearly penniless. The year was 1937. César was only ten years old.

BECOMING MIGRANT

Librado thought he might find work on the huge farms in California. Hoping for the best, he packed his family, some clothes, and a few blankets into an old car and headed west. The little group soon joined a horde of homeless people in California.

For the next ten years, the Chávezes were **migrant workers**. In the fields, the whole family hand-tended and hand-harvested peas, corn, strawberries, walnuts, melons, beans, tomatoes, grapes, cotton, lettuce, and more. Even the youngest children became expert at planting, weeding, and picking. When the work ended, the family packed up and made their way to another part of the state. If they wanted to survive, they had to go where work could be found.

The Dust Bowl and the Okies

In the early 1930s, the south-central United States experienced the worst drought in its history. Without rain, the crops died and the wind blew the topsoil away. Farmers could no longer raise crops to sell or eat, and their families began to starve. Hoping to find work and food, many headed to the huge commercial farms in the western and south-western United States. States like California and Texas were soon home to thousands of extremely poor men, women, and children. Others who were more fortunate sometimes disparagingly called these starving, homeless people "Okies" because many came from Oklahoma.

The south-central region of the United States became known as the Dust Bowl after severe drought and over-farming ruined the land.

Dishonest labor contractors often tried to take advantage of Librado and Juana Chávez by underpaying them for the work they did or not paying at all. But the couple always stood up for themselves. According to César, "Our mother used to say there is a difference between being of service and being a servant." She did not let growers or contractors cheat her out of her money, even though they often retaliated by firing the whole family and kicking them off their ranches. César proudly remembered that "when she wasn't helping people or getting us fired for challenging labor contractors, we were the strikingest family in all of farm labor. Whenever we were working where there was a **strike** or when the workers got fed up and walked off the job, she'd be the first one to back up our dad's decision to join the strike. Our mother taught us not to be afraid to fight—to stand up for our rights. But she also taught us not to be violent."

These boys have been harvesting cotton all day. When César was their age, he spent most of his days the same way.

Juana Chávez was a devout Roman Catholic who felt a deep responsibility to help others. Long after he was grown up, César recalled that "as poor as we were, and with what little we had, mama would send my brother Richard and me out to railroad yards and other places for 'hobos' we could invite to our tent to share a meal. . . . Our mother would tell us, 'You always help the needy, and God will help you.'"

Librado and Juana Chávez could not read or write, but they wanted their children to attend school. Unfortunately, the kids were never in the same school for long because the family moved so often. One after another, those schools provided a miserable experience for César. Some of the other children and even the teachers criticized him for speaking Spanish and for making mistakes in English. They treated him as if he was "stupid" just because he was a Mexican American. César never forgot the cruelty and prejudice he suffered

A Tough Winter

According to Chávez, "One winter we were stranded in Oxnard and had to spend the winter in a tent. We were the only people there living in a tent and everyone ridiculed us. We went to bed at dusk because there was no light. My mother and father got up at 5:30 in the morning to go pick peas. It cost seventy cents to go to the fields and back, and some days they did not even make enough for their transportation. To help out, my brother and I started looking along the highway for empty cigarette packages, for the tinfoil. Every day we would look for cigarette packages, and we made a huge ball of tinfoil that weighed eighteen pounds. Then we sold it to a Mexican junk dealer for enough money to buy a pair of tennis shoes and two sweatshirts."

in those schools. He once recalled that "we were like monkeys in a cage. There were lots of racist remarks that still hurt my ears when I think of them. And we couldn't do anything except sit there and take it."

Shortly after César finished the eighth grade, Librado was hurt in a car crash. Since his father could not work for some time, César decided to drop out of school and work like a grown man to support the family. His mother wanted him to stay in school, but he refused. In 1942, at the age of fifteen, the boy left school and became a full-time field worker. He worked on farms all over California for the next two years, but his family continued to live in abject poverty.

In 1944, César joined the navy. He hoped to help the United States and its allies win World War II, but he soon learned that he would not be allowed to fight. Instead, he and most other Mexican-American service-men were stuck painting ships and cleaning the decks. **Discrimination**, he discovered, was as common in the armed forces as it was in rural California.

César graduated from eighth grade in 1942. After that, he worked in the fields full-time to support his family.

CHAPTER 3

LEARNING TO ORGANIZE

When the war and his term of service ended, César was glad to leave the navy. He returned to California, where he fell in love with a farm worker's daughter who wore flowers in her hair and loved to dance. Helen Fabela and César had met years earlier in a malt shop, and they had dated for a while before he joined the navy. They married in 1948 and moved into a one-room shack in Delano, not far from Helen's family. As they began to have children, however, the couple found that the vineyards and cotton fields around Delano did not offer enough work to support them. Out of necessity, they hit the road in search of work. The family traveled the West Coast for the next two years, going wherever César could find temporary jobs.

In 1952, they moved to San Jose, California, where César was able to find work in a lumber mill. Unfortunately, the pay was low and the work was part time, so the Chávezes were still barely able to get by. César, his pregnant wife, and their three children lived in a grim part of southeast San Jose called Sal Si Puedes. In English the name means "get out if you can"— an appropriate name for a slum filled with dilapidated shacks and muddy, unpaved roads. Sanitation in Sal Si Puedes was poor, and the people who lived there were even poorer.

Like the slum shown in this photo, Sal Si Puedes was filled with mud, trash, and shacks.

On the miserable streets of Sal Si Puedes, Chávez met two men who changed his life. The first was Father Donald McDonnell, a Catholic priest and **social activist**. Chávez later said that McDonnell "told me about social justice, and the Church's stand on farm labor and . . . labor unions. I would do anything to get the Father to tell more about labor history. I began going to the **bracero** camps with him to help with the mass, to the city jail with him to talk to the prisoners, anything to be with him."

Braceros

During World War II, with so many men in the military, the United States went through a labor shortage. The federal government decided to bring in Mexicans to work in the fields. Called *braceros*, which is Spanish for "a pair of arms," these laborers were transported to the United States by the busload. They worked for low wages, did not complain, and were sent back home when they were no longer needed. Pleased with this program, growers convinced the Labor Department to continue it after the war ended. Supposedly, the government set standards to ensure decent treatment of braceros, but in reality they lived and worked in appalling conditions.

This car is packed full of braceros. Photographed in 1943, they are coming to the United States to harvest sugar beets.

Under the priest's guidance, César began to read. He struggled through books about the lives of saints, labor leaders, and freedom fighters. He was especially captivated by biographies of Mahatma Gandhi, an East Indian leader whose spirituality, passion, and commitment to nonviolence stirred César's heart and mind.

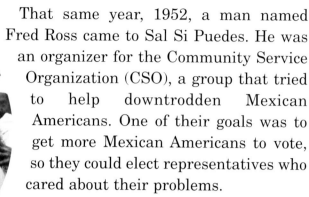

Mahatma Gandhi (right) believed in the power of nonviolent resistance. Using only peaceful means, Gandhi led India to freedom from British rule in 1947.

That same year, 1952, a man named Fred Ross came to Sal Si Puedes. He was an organizer for the Community Service Organization (CSO), a group that tried to help downtrodden Mexican Americans. One of their goals was to get more Mexican Americans to vote, so they could elect representatives who cared about their problems.

Ross was from Los Angeles, and he needed someone in Sal Si Puedes to handle the local voter registration drive. Several people, including Father McDonnell, suggested that he talk to César Chávez. César, however, did not want to talk to him. He was sure that Ross did not really know anything about the problems of the campesinos. Unwilling to meet with Ross, César managed to slip away whenever the CSO representative came to his house.

Helen finally convinced César to stay home and listen to Fred Ross. Years later, Ross remembered that first meeting quite well: "I told César . . . I had worked all over Southern California and wherever I went the conditions among the Mexican Americans were as bad as in Sal Si Puedes. The same polluted creeks . . . for kids to play in. The same kind of cops beating up young guys. . . . The same mean streets and walkways and lack of streetlights and traffic signals. The same poor drainage, overflowing cesspools, and [disease]. . . . César was impressed: I knew his problems as well as anyone."

EARLY VOLUNTEER WORK

Indeed, Chávez was impressed, so impressed that he volunteered to work with the CSO. Soon he was knock-

ing on doors in poor neighborhoods and talking to complete strangers. He helped many Mexican immigrants apply for U.S. citizenship, and he urged them to register to vote. César was still terribly shy, but he threw himself into his volunteer work anyway.

These years were important ones for César Chávez. "I began to grow and to see a lot of things that I hadn't seen before," he recalled. "My eyes opened, and I paid more attention to political and social events." During this time, he began to think that farm workers did not have to stay trapped in an endless cycle of poverty and despair. In addition, Chávez came to believe that the campesinos did not necessarily need charity or large sums of money to improve their lives. If they worked together, he believed, they could solve their problems without outside help.

While he lived in Sal Si Puedes, Chávez also learned the importance of organizing people so they could work effectively as a group. Looking back on the early 1950s, Chávez recalled, "All the time I was observing the things Fred did, secretly, because I wanted to learn how to organize, to see how it was done. . . . I was impressed with his patience, and understanding of people. I thought this was a tool, one of the greatest things he had."

This group of CSO organizers posed for the camera in 1954. In the front row, Fred Ross is in the center and César is second from the right. Helen Chávez is third from the right in the back row.

SETTING UP NEW CHAPTERS

In 1952, Fred Ross, César Chávez, and the other CSO volunteers registered six thousand new voters in the Delano area. A short time later, when Chávez was laid off at the lumber mill, the CSO directors offered him a

Being Branded a Communist

Many people were suspicious of Ross and Chávez's efforts to work with farm laborers. Some even accused Chávez of being a **communist** and trying to subvert the American way of life. Especially in the 1950s, when tensions between the United States and the **Soviet Union** were on the rise and fear of communism ran high, being called a communist often led to trouble. People sometimes lost their friends, reputations, and jobs after being accused, even when the accusations were absurd. From the 1950s on, the FBI repeatedly investigated César Chávez. Each time the investigators concluded that he was not a communist sympathizer. Instead, he was just what he seemed to be—a man who cared passionately about field workers.

In the 1950s, Senator Joseph McCarthy led a nationwide hunt for communists. His wild accusations ruined the lives and careers of many U.S. citizens.

full-time job as an organizer. The salary was only $35 a week, but César thought the work was worthwhile, so he was happy to accept.

The Sal Si Puedes chapter was doing well, and the CSO was eager to start other chapters. Soon after César became a paid employee, Fred Ross asked him to go to Oakland and organize a new chapter there.

The Oakland assignment was quite a challenge. César was a stranger to the city, and he had trouble finding his way around. Nevertheless, he started holding "house meetings," where people volunteered their homes as meeting places and whoever was interested could attend. The first few meetings in Oakland were excruciating for the shy new organizer. To his amazement and delight, however, people not only came to the meetings, but they listened and responded enthusiastically! In fact, just months after arriving in Oakland,

Chávez was ready to hold a big meeting at a church. When hundreds of people attended, it became clear that he was extraordinarily good at his new job.

After his success in Oakland, Chávez was asked to organize chapters elsewhere in California. He and his family moved from place to place, depending on César's current assignment. Of all the places he went, the town of Oxnard probably offered the most exciting challenge. When he arrived there in 1958, he found that local laborers were not being hired to work in the fields. Instead, growers were importing braceros to work for less money, even though it was illegal for growers to hire braceros when there were local field workers available.

César saw it as his duty to help. He started by documenting the local workers' attempts to register for work. When he could prove that they were being turned away in favor of braceros, he contacted government officials, organized **picket lines** of local workers, and did whatever he could to embarrass the growers. Before

Chávez (far right) and the other CSO volunteers helped thousands of poor people register to vote.

A house meeting in Oakland

A local priest set up César's first house meeting in Oakland. The only participants were a few women. Chávez felt too uncomfortable to speak, so for a long time he did not say a word. One of the women finally asked when the CSO man would arrive. Then Chávez had to admit that he was the representative. He later reported that the "meeting was a disaster, really a disaster. I fumbled all over the place. . . . But toward the end of the meeting they were listening to me, and I got them to promise to hold . . . a lot of house meetings and to commit themselves."

long, the growers gave in and hired a few locals. Then government officials forced the growers to hire local workers consistently. César's strategy had worked. It was his first success at organizing workers to protest unfair practices. He wrote to Fred Ross, "This has been a wonderful experience . . . for me. I never dreamed that so much hell could be raised."

In this 1959 photo, Mexican cotton workers wait for their pay. When payday came, field workers were at the mercy of their bosses. Sometimes the workers were underpaid, and sometimes they were not paid at all.

EXECUTIVE DIRECTOR

The upper management of the CSO asked César Chávez to become the group's executive director in 1959. It was a choice that paid off well. With Chávez in charge, the CSO grew to twenty-two chapters and became the most effective Mexican-American **civil rights** group in the United States.

As successful as the CSO was, César was not satisfied. He wanted to focus more on the needs of the field workers. In 1962, he proposed that the CSO start officially organizing farm laborers "to end the exploitation of the workers in the fields," he said, ". . . to strike at the roots of their suffering and poverty." The directors liked his proposal, but the general membership did not. They wanted to concentrate on problems in cities, not in farm country, so they rejected his proposal.

Chávez was not ready to drop the idea. Rather than turn away from the field workers, he decided to resign from the CSO and strike out more or less on his own. He was determined to start a farm workers' union, with or without the CSO's backing.

BUILDING THE NFWA

When Chávez left the CSO in March 1962, he moved his family back to Delano, California. He chose Delano for two reasons. First, both he and Helen had relatives there, and César wanted to be near family. Second, the town was in a large fertile valley where thousands of campesinos lived and worked. The laborers César hoped to organize were all around him.

Starting a union was a full-time job. Unfortunately, it did not provide a paycheck or feed the Chávez children. "For the first time," César recalled, "I was frightened—I was very frightened." Fortunately for the family, friends and relatives helped feed and clothe them while Chávez threw himself into organizing workers.

A NEW APPROACH

César knew that field laborers desperately needed to change their lives but were suspicious of unions. In the past, attempts to unionize them had led to strikes, violence, short-lived pay raises, firings, and—in the end—no change in the awful working conditions, unreliable work, and pitifully low pay. Many people agreed with the farm worker who told Chávez, "They come and they go, good organizers and would-be organizers. But one thing they all have in common is that all of them have failed and all will fail."

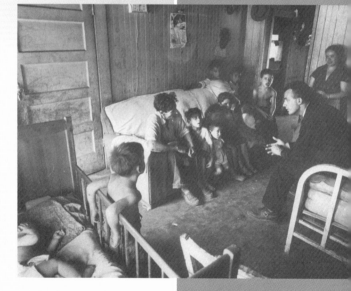

A dedicated priest visits a migrant family in 1959. Even the most well-meaning people did not know how to help the field workers help themselves.

César had another problem, too: it was illegal for farm hands to join a labor union. Therefore, if the local growers found out about his efforts to organize workers, they would undoubtedly call the police. Given the illegal nature of his work and its negative associations for field laborers, he decided to call the new group an "association" rather than a union.

Chávez had very definite ideas about how a really good farm workers' "association" should operate. First, in terms of membership, leadership, and funding, it should be a **grassroots** organization—one in which the members themselves had the will, the ability, and the patience to do whatever it took to be successful. The group must depend on the workers themselves, not on big-shot leaders in far-away offices. And it must fund its own activities and turn down money from outsiders who might use their contributions to influence the group's activities.

He told field workers they did not need people to give them money. "We have the other ingredient, which is more important than money," he said, "and that is time." Time, patience, and determination would be their advantages. According to one of César's organizing associates, "he often said time will accomplish for the poor what money does for the rich."

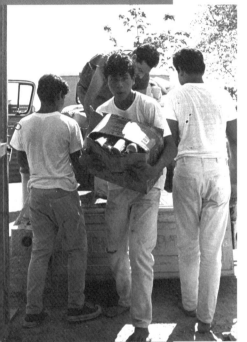

Friends and supporters donated food to the Chávez family so César could focus on organizing the workers. In this photo, volunteers carry food donated to members of the National Farm Workers Association (NFWA) during their strike against grape growers.

GAINING ONE MEMBER AT A TIME

The fledgling association started with only three members—César, Helen, and Dolores Huerta, an extremely capable organizer who had worked with César at the CSO. Their first activity was to gather information. They printed up a short questionnaire on index cards, asking only for a farm worker's name, address, and opinions about issues such as how much they should be paid. Next, the organizers identified eighty-six key farming towns in the valley and began distributing their questionnaires. They left piles of them at grocery stores and on bulletin boards at labor camps—anywhere they thought field laborers might see them. Taking their young children with them, they also visited campesinos in their homes. Through thousands of conversations that happened during their sixteen- to eighteen-hour days, César, Helen, and Dolores learned firsthand about the workers' lives. Over and over, they explained to laborers the value of working together to solve problems and asked them to join their organization. "From the depth of need and despair," César told the workers he met, "people can work together, can organize themselves to solve their own problems and fill their own needs with dignity and strength."

César Chávez knew the importance of being a good listener. Dozens of people told him their stories every day

Personal Relationships Help Build a Union

In 1963 a field worker named Manuel Rivera came to Chávez for help. His car had fallen apart, his family had nowhere to live, and he was having trouble with an unreasonable boss. Chávez was happy to help. He lent Rivera his own battered old car, took the family into his home, and later helped them find a car and a place of their own. When Rivera tried to pay him for all he had done, César suggested that he help the local farm workers instead. Rivera enthusiastically joined the NFWA and soon brought in dozens of new members. According to a minister who worked with Chávez, "That's how [César's] union was built: on plain hard work and these very personal relationships. It was a slow, careful, plodding thing. . . . He simply built up this basic trust."

Like César, Dolores Huerta worked ceaselessly on behalf of the farm workers.

As César expected, many people were not interested. A few, however, were very enthusiastic. Finally, after about six months of recruiting, they had enough interest to hold a founding convention. The group met on September 20, 1962, in Fresno, California. At the meeting, they voted to call themselves the National Farm Workers Association (NFWA) and charge monthly dues of $3.50. The members also agreed on a motto—"¡Viva la causa!" ("Long live the cause!")—and a design for an NFWA flag. They elected César Chávez president and voted to **lobby** growers for a minimum wage of $1.50 per hour.

The newly formed NFWA began addressing field workers' problems at once. One common concern was that they could rarely get bank loans. To address that need, César Chávez bought a book on accounting and learned how to set up a credit union for NFWA members. He even convinced his brother Richard to mortgage his house so the NFWA would have a few thousand dollars to lend. His creative approach showed many people that farm workers could indeed solve some of their own problems.

While César was working hard with the NFWA, Helen and the older children were working in the fields to support their family. When money was especially tight, César joined them there. Even then, however, his work for the union never stopped. One NFWA member

The NFWA flag featured an eagle because Chávez believed that the eagle "gives pride. . . . When people see it they know it means dignity." The wings had squared edges that would be easy to draw and sew when people made their own flags.

El Malcriado

In December 1964, the NFWA began publishing its own newspaper. Chávez named the paper *El Malcriado*, which means "the brat" or "the child who speaks back to his parents." At first, the articles were written in Spanish—a language many workers but very few growers could read. Free from the prying eyes of the growers, *El Malcriado*'s editors could write without restraint. They demanded decent wages, blasted the unfair practices of the growers, and called for farm laborers to work together for change. The newspaper was very popular with field workers and helped spread the NFWA's ideas.

described a typical day for César and himself this way: "We'd begin [putting out leaflets] before the roosters got up, around three in the morning. Then we'd go to work, and then we'd get back to passing out information, until well after dark." It was exhausting but exhilarating work.

CHAPTER 5

¡HUELGA! ¡HUELGA!

Right from the start, almost everyone César Chávez talked to about the NFWA asked whether there would be strikes. "I have been saying—no strikes," he wrote, "unless we know we'll win." Chávez was a patient man. He was willing to wait for the organization to grow big enough and the workers' resolve to grow strong enough to beat the powerful growers. The workers themselves, however, were not as patient.

THE GREAT DELANO GRAPE STRIKE

By 1965, many field workers in the San Joaquin Valley felt angry and frustrated. Their frustration came to a head on September 8, the day **Filipino** laborers struck local grape growers to protest a wage cut. The growers fought back by cutting off electricity in the labor camps and bringing in "scabs"—replacements who would work in the fields while the regular workers were on strike. The growers had money and power, and they were sure they could outwit and outlast the striking workers. They thought the strikers would return to work when they got hungry enough.

The Filipino workers' organization—called the Agricultural Workers Organizing Committee (AWOC)—knew it needed help from other workers. Turning to César Chávez and the NFWA, they asked for support. President Chávez called for a general meeting of the NFWA on September 16. Word of the meeting was spread through a special edition of *El Malcriado*, and the editors urged all local farm workers to attend. The editors also stated their own opinions in no uncertain terms: "Now is when every worker, without regard to race, color, and nationality, should support the strike and under no circumstances work in those ranches that have been struck."

The NFWA's general meeting was well-attended. Emotions ran high as numerous working men and women spoke about the humiliations they had suffered on the job. One after another, they urged other members to vote for a strike.

Chávez addressed the crowd, too. He said the workers were involved in a "struggle for the freedom and dignity which poverty denies us." Wanting everyone to be realistic, however, he warned that strikers would get no wages until they returned to work. He also reminded the campesinos that once they went on strike they had to continue to strike until the growers met their demands—and that could take a very long time.

Chávez asked the members to decide what they wanted to do. As cries of "*¡Viva la causa!*" and "*¡Huelga! ¡Huelga!*" ("Strike! Strike!") rocked the hall, the NFWA workers voted to demand the same wages as the AWOC workers and strike until their demands were met. By the end of the meeting, the AWOC and the NFWA were jointly on strike against forty-eight ranches. The Great Delano Grape Strike had begun.

Strikers met early each morning outside one or more ranches. They were not allowed on the growers' land, so they

When these field workers voted to strike, they made an important statement: no longer would they cooperate with growers who mistreated them.

The strikers called to scabs, "¡Huelga! ¡Huelga! Join us in the fight for fair wages!" Many scabs dropped their tools and joined the strike.

Dr. Martin Luther King, Jr., was a passionate and persuasive speaker.

gathered on the nearby roadside. All day long they held picket signs and urged scabs to stop working. Many of the scabs left the fields and joined the picket lines.

The growers were annoyed, but they had seen short-term strikes before and thought they knew how to handle the situation. They harassed the pickets—kicking and elbowing them, swearing at them, "buzzing" them with cars and trucks—doing whatever they could to cause trouble. They hoped to incite the strikers to violence, make them step onto a grower's land, or otherwise break the law. Meanwhile, the local police stood nearby, waiting to arrest the workers for real or perceived infractions. They rarely arrested the growers or their foremen, however, even when one ran over a striker with a truck.

Martin Luther King, Jr.

In the 1960s, the African American Civil Rights Movement was making headlines. The leader of that movement, Dr. Martin Luther King, Jr., was a brilliant and persuasive orator whose speeches inspired millions to protest the racial segregation and discrimination that blacks had suffered since slavery was abolished in 1865. King believed in the power of nonviolent resistance. He spearheaded the 1963 March on Washington and other enormously successful peaceful protests. The success of his nonviolent tactics impressed and inspired César Chávez, who adapted them for the farm workers' fight for equality.

César Chávez often reminded the pickets that they must not meet violence from the growers with violence of their own. "Violence can only hurt us and our cause," he told them. "Instead of exposing the brutality of the oppressor, it justifies it." When tensions ran especially high, President Chávez brought priests and ministers to the picket lines, and their presence helped the workers stay calm. Thanks to these efforts and a great deal of self-control, very few strikers physically fought back.

Most strikers remained peaceful even when they were provoked.

Chávez knew that the strikers needed to get public opinion on their side in order to influence the growers. With that need in mind, he began visiting churches and universities, talking with everyone who seemed interested. He asked for and received help from many groups. One important ally was the Student Nonviolent Coordinating Committee (SNCC), a nationwide organi-

El Teatro Campesino

Luis Valdez was a young actor who cared deeply about civil rights. In 1965, he tracked down Chávez in Oakland and asked his permission to start a street theater troupe in Delano. He told César that, by putting on funny skits, the workers could entertain themselves and educate people about la causa. Chávez agreed, and *El Teatro Campesino* ("The Farm Workers' Theater") was formed. The little theater group was an instant success and a valuable addition to the strikers' arsenal of nonviolent weapons. Using the back of a flatbed truck as a stage, the workers-turned-actors performed wickedly funny satires about evil growers who only pretended to care about field workers. Their clever skits attracted many new members and supporters to the cause.

The growers tried to fight back with signs of their own, but they did not get much sympathy from the general public.

zation of college students that promoted civil rights. With the help of the SNCC, Chávez spread word of the field workers' cause from state to state.

In another bold and ingenious move, Chávez broadened the area of the strike. He sent NFWA members to Los Angeles and San Francisco to picket grape warehouses and loading docks. Many workers in those cities supported the strikers and refused to cross the picket lines.

In December 1965, Chávez and the NFWA-AWOC coalition ratcheted up the pressure another notch: they announced a boycott of products made by Schenley Industries, a huge liquor company that happened to own a few vineyards in California. Working with the SNCC and various church-based groups, Chávez and his people reached out to thousands and asked them to participate in the boycott. Soon, people all over the United States were refusing to buy Schenley products. Despite mounting public pressure, however, the giant corporation refused to negotiate.

Chávez and the other NFWA and AWOC leaders kept finding new ways to embarrass and pressure the growers. One of their best ideas was to undertake a long, very public march. The *perigrinación* ("pilgrimage"), as César called it, was to cover almost 350 miles (563 kilometers), the distance from Delano to the state capital in Sacramento. Once in Sacramento, they would present their case to Governor Edmund Brown.

On March 17, 1966, the march began. That morning, many TV, newspaper, and magazine cameramen were on hand as Chávez, Dolores Huerta, and sixty-seven field workers started walking north. Video cameras rolled, shutters snapped, and the perigrinación was underway.

The march lasted more than three weeks. Some of the original participants dropped out, but dozens more joined as the workers passed through one town after another. Angie Hernandez Herrera was one of the *originales*—those who walked the full distance. "Some people had bloody feet," she recalled. "Some would keep walking and you'd see blood coming out of their shoes." Despite the pain, the marchers' spirits were high. In every town, sympathetic locals offered food and shelter. There were rallies and celebrations in support of the workers' cause almost every day.

Finally, when the marchers were only a few days away from the capital, Schenley surprised everyone by announcing that the company would recognize the NFWA as the field workers' representative and would give workers a raise of thirty-five cents per hour. This was amazing news. It meant the NFWA had won! Schenley kept its word. A few weeks later, in June 1966, the company's lawyers and the NFWA signed a labor contract—the first ever negotiated between growers and farm workers in the continental United States.

By the time Chávez (far left) reached Sacramento, his feet were so blistered and his legs so swollen that he could barely walk.

CHAPTER 6

THE UNION MATURES

The signing of the Schenley contract was a tremendous breakthrough for the field workers, but it was really only a first step in the fight for fair treatment. Most growers still refused to increase wages or improve working conditions, and most refused to negotiate with or recognize the NFWA.

After the AWOC and NFWA became the UFWOC, the strikes and boycotts continued.

THE NFWOC IS BORN

In August 1966, the AWOC and the NFWA merged to form the United Farm Workers Organizing Committee (UFWOC), a new union that existed under the auspices of the American Federation of Labor and Congress of Industrial Organizations (AFL-CIO). The UFWOC elected Chávez as director and Larry Itliong, the former head of the AWOC, as assistant director. In the new organization, field workers continued to organize strikes, boycotts, and work slowdowns as they pressed California's grape growers and processors to give them a fair deal.

Those activities kept la causa in the national headlines and kept public sympathy solidly behind the field workers. By 1968, many labor unions, civil rights organizations, church groups, and concerned politicians, along with hundreds of thousands of students and ordinary housewives, were supporting the workers. As a result of a nationwide boycott, millions of people in the United States had stopped buying grapes.

Throughout those years, picketing and demonstrating were dangerous jobs because the growers and their supporters had no qualms about resorting to violence. They threatened and taunted strikers, beat them up, and "buzzed" them with trucks. Police who were sympathetic to the growers arrested and jailed dozens of field workers, including Chávez, more than once. Despite this unfair treatment and abuse, Director Chávez maintained that meeting violence with violence was wrong and that nonviolence was a sign of greater inner strength. "Nonviolence," he said, "is not for the timid or

César and Helen Chávez with six of their seven children in the late 1960s

Living with César Chávez

It was not easy being the child of César Chávez. His daughter Eloise remembers having problems at school with growers' children. According to Eloise, they "would tell us how we were rich, that our father had a private jet, a big bank account in Switzerland and a mansion in Acapulco." The truth was that César received only $5.00 from the union each week. His family of ten lived in a tiny, broken-down two-bedroom house and usually ate rice and beans that had been donated by relatives, union members, and supporters.

Despite the poverty in which they lived and their father's frequent absences from home, all eight children were devoted to la causa. Linda Chávez, for example, wore "Boycott Grapes" buttons to school and once refused to cross a picket line when her class went on a field trip to a raisin-packing plant. Although her teacher threatened to have her expelled, Linda returned to the bus and sat there while the rest of the class learned how grapes are made into raisins.

weak. . . . Nonviolence is hard work." Instead of violence, he advocated a continued policy of non-cooperation. "The first principle of non-violent action," he announced, "is that of non-cooperation with everything humiliating."

THE FIRST FAST

Despite César's pleas for patience and restraint, many UFWOC members began to lose faith in their leader's approach. As time went on, there was more and more talk about resorting to physical force. Chávez was appalled by this talk. Cursing in frustration, he once shouted at the UFWOC directors, "Goddamn it! We'll never be able to get anywhere if we start using tactics of violence. . . . You have to believe in that!"

To encourage his fellow workers to recommit to nonviolence, César decided to show the depth of his own commitment and willingness to sacrifice. Inspired by Mahatma Gandhi, who had fasted decades earlier to protest British rule over India, he decided to undertake an extended fast.

Sometimes the union's problems must have seemed almost over-whelming to César.

Chávez stopped eating on February 15, 1968. At first, almost no one noticed. Then, at a meeting on February 19, he announced that he would not eat again until the union reaffirmed its commitment to nonviolence. Some of his associates and followers thought he was crazy. Helen—usually his biggest supporter—told him he was being ridicu-

Telegram from Dr. Martin Luther King, Jr.

César Chávez and Martin Luther King, Jr., never met but they supported each other's efforts. Dr. King sent the following telegram to Chávez during his fast in 1968.

"I am deeply moved by your courage in fasting as your personal sacrifice for justice through nonviolence. Your past and present commitment is eloquent testimony to the constructive power of nonviolent action and the destructive impotence of violent reprisal. You stand today as a living example of . . . [this] great force for social progress and its healing spiritual powers. My colleagues and I commend you for your bravery, salute you for your indefatigable work against poverty and injustice, and pray for your health and your continuing service as one of the outstanding men of America. The plight of your people and ours is so grave that we all desperately need the inspiring example and effective leadership you have given."

Martin Luther King, Jr.

President

SCLC

lous. Others worried that their leader would starve to death. But no one could convince Chávez to eat.

Days went by. Chávez lost weight. He soon became too weak to work and remained at home. Then, in a series of unexpected developments, people began visiting his house to talk, to show their support and concern, or just to be near him. Furthermore, the news media started reporting on the fast, donations to the UFWOC poured in, and European dock workers refused to unload American grapes that arrived by ship. In response to

Senator Robert Kennedy sits with César as the union leader ends his three-week-long fast.

César's prolonged act of self-denial, public sympathy for la causa grew stronger.

After three weeks of fasting and talking with union members and supporters, Chávez announced that his fast had served its purpose. A celebration was held on March 11. Thousands of people attended, including Senator Robert Kennedy. Calling Chávez "one of the heroic figures of our time," Kennedy shared a piece of bread with the labor leader. It was the first food Chávez had eaten in twenty-five days.

VICTORY

After César's fast, UFWOC members felt a renewed sense of commitment and hope, so they continued to rely on nonviolent tactics. Their patience and persistence finally paid off in the summer of 1970, when most of the major grape growers in California agreed to the union's demands. They signed labor contracts guaranteeing higher pay, health insurance, and other benefits to workers.

At one of the contract signings, Chávez spoke to the assembled growers and workers. "Without the help of those millions upon millions of people who believe as we do that nonviolence is the way to struggle," he told them, "I'm sure that we wouldn't be here today. The strikers and the people involved in this struggle sacrificed a lot. . . . Ninety-five percent of the strikers lost their homes and their cars. But I think in losing those worldly possessions, they found themselves." The room rang with shouts and applause as the workers expressed their joy. They celebrated the contract, but they also celebrated something even more important—the gains they had made in self-respect during those five long, hard years of nonviolent confrontation.

Victory at last! A contract is signed in 1970, after five long years of strikes and boycotts.

CHAPTER 7

THE FIGHT CONTINUES

The agreements signed with growers in 1970 represented a high point for César Chávez, the UFWOC, and California's field workers. Unfortunately, it was not one they were able to maintain.

TWO UNIONS DUKE IT OUT

Soon after these historic signings, vegetable growers across California undercut the union's power in a crafty move. They signed labor agreements with the International Brotherhood of Teamsters, a rough-and-tumble union that did not truly represent the workers' interests. The growers knew the Teamsters would not pressure them to guarantee jobs, wages, and better working conditions for field laborers. In fact, the contracts they signed with the Teamsters were quite unfavorable to the workers.

Three years later, in 1973, when the UFWOC's contracts with the grape growers came up for renewal, these growers also signed with the Teamsters. Then they told grape workers that if they wanted jobs, they had to join the Teamsters. Infuriated, thousands of grape workers walked off their jobs. Tensions between the competing unions ran high, and there were numerous clashes. Beatings, arrests, and even murders followed.

As the violence escalated, it was harder and harder for Chávez to convince people that "we do not need to kill or destroy to win." He spent thousands of hours trying to keep people calm while fending off the challenge by the Teamsters over who should represent the field

The Great Lettuce War

When California lettuce growers signed contracts with the Teamsters Union in 1970, over ten thousand angry field workers went on strike. It was the largest strike of farm workers in history. Seeking support for the strikers, Chávez called for a nationwide boycott of lettuce. When a local court ordered him to call off the boycott, he refused and was sent to jail. He stayed in jail for two weeks before another court ordered him to be released. Commenting on those two weeks, Chávez reportedly said, "My spirit was never in jail. They can jail us, but they can never jail la causa." The boycott continued for many years. It ended only after most California lettuce growers signed UFW contracts that were favorable to the workers.

Thousands of people wore these pins to show their support for the lettuce boycott.

workers. Distracted by this struggle, Chávez became less effective in negotiations with the growers even though he was working eighteen-hour days. Many workers lost faith in César's methods and leadership during this period, and membership in the UFWOC declined.

The Teamsters began to weaken in 1976, but it was not until the following year that they surrendered. After that, the UFWOC (renamed the United Farm Workers or UFW in 1973) was once again the main organizing force in the fields, and César Chávez could devote himself to bargaining with growers on behalf of the campesinos.

In the mid-1970s, the UFW won most of the union elections it entered. Membership soared, and within just a few years many thousands of farm workers were

The Agricultural Labor Relations Act

Despite the problems with the Teamsters, Chávez and the UFW scored some major successes during the mid-1970s. With 17 million Americans boycotting grapes, the California legislature finally took positive action. They drafted and passed the Agricultural Labor Relations Bill. Governor Jerry Brown, a Democrat and a staunch ally of unions, made history when he signed the bill into law in 1975.

California's Agricultural Labor Relations Act was the first law ever passed in the United States that guaranteed rights for agricultural workers. It gave farm laborers the legal right to organize and collectively bargain with their employers. To ensure fairness, it also provided for government supervision at the bargaining table.

receiving higher pay, health insurance, pensions, and increased job security, thanks to their UFW contracts.

THE GROWERS WIN A ROUND

Despite the successes of the UFW, California's growers were not ready to stop fighting. During the gubernatorial campaign of 1982, they contributed enormous sums of money (over a million dollars) to the Republican candidate, George Deukmejian. Soon after he won the election, state officials stopped enforcing pro-labor laws, and many UFW members lost their jobs and were blacklisted by growers. Despite the illegality of these actions, Chávez and the UFW were not able to muster enough political support to correct the situation. The growers were delighted.

About that same time, the public began to lose interest in labor issues. Chávez's boycotts and marches

Fred Ross (second from left) and César (second from right) remained close for many years. When Fred died in 1992, César delivered the eulogy at the funeral.

then lost some of their effectiveness, and many key UFW members chafed under César's use of tactics that did not seem to work. In the early 1980s, some of the union's best organizers left the organization over differences in leadership style and tactics.

LAST YEARS

César was frustrated but not deterred. "All my life," he said, "I have been driven by one dream, one goal, one vision: To overthrow a farm labor system in this nation which treats farm workers as if they were not important human beings. Farm workers are not agricultural implements. They are not beasts of burden—to be used and discarded." With these thoughts in

Family Matters

All of César and Helen's children remained committed to la Causa and worked for field laborers' rights after they grew up. Linda Chávez, the third child in the family, married a union worker named Arturo Rodriguez in 1974. When César died nineteen years later, Arturo became the UFW's second president. He still serves in that capacity today.

César protested the use of pesticides that poisoned workers and caused severe birth defects in their children.

mind, César remained at the helm of the UFW and continued his nonviolent fight for the rights of workers.

Chávez and his remaining supporters worked hard throughout the 1980s, trying to regain the ground they had lost. In 1986, César led a campaign called the "Wrath of Grapes" to protest the use of deadly pesticides in the fields. Then, two years later, he undertook a water-only "Fast for Life." Greatly weakened after thirty-six days without food, he passed the fast along to civil rights activist Jesse Jackson. Jackson fasted for three days and then passed the fast on to other leaders and celebrities, each of whom fasted for three days to draw public attention to the dangers of pesticides.

César Chávez died in his sleep on April 23, 1993. He was sixty-six years old. In all those years, he never owned a house or a car, and he never made more than $900 a month. His work was his passion, and he expected little in the way of **tangible** rewards. "True wealth is not measured in money or status or power," he said more than once. "It is measured by the legacy that we leave behind for those we love and those we inspire." For field workers who now have a union and who continue to fight for their rights, the legacy left behind by César Chávez is immense.

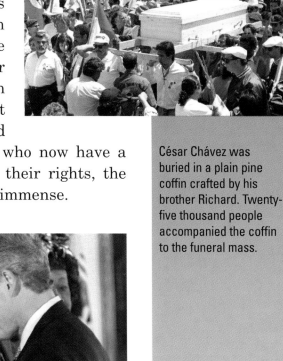

César Chávez was buried in a plain pine coffin crafted by his brother Richard. Twenty-five thousand people accompanied the coffin to the funeral mass.

In 1994, President Bill Clinton awarded the Presidential Medal of Freedom to César Chávez **posthumously**. Helen Chávez accepted the medal in her husband's place.

TIMELINE

1927	César Estrada Chávez is born on March 31
1937	Chávez family forced to leave their farm; become migrant workers
1942	César graduates from eighth grade. Begins working in the fields full-time
1948	Marries Helen Fabela
1952	Joins the Community Service Organization (CSO)
1962	Resigns as National Director of the CSO. Founds the National Farm Worker's Association (NFWA) in Fresno, California on September 30
1965	Leads the NFWA and the Agricultural Workers Organizing Committee (AWOC) in striking against forth-eight California grape ranches
1966	With dozens of supporters, marches 350 miles (563 km) from Delano to Sacramento to publicize unfair treatment of field workers
1968	Fasts for twenty-five days to strengthen the UFW's commitment to nonviolence
1970	Signs the first contracts for farm workers in the continental United States. Calls for a nationwide boycott of lettuce to protest vegetable growers' contracts with the Teamsters Union
1973	Against the wishes of farm workers, grape growers sign deals with Teamsters
1975	Chávez calls a halt to boycotts against grape and lettuce growers
1988	Fasts for thirty-six days to draw attention to children who are dying of cancer because of pesticides used on grapes
1993	Dies in his sleep in San Luis, Arizona, on April 23
1994	U.S. president Bill Clinton posthumously awards the Presidential Medal of Freedom to César Chávez. César's widow, Helen, accepts the medal
1994	March 31 is designated César Chávez day in California

GLOSSARY

braceros: Mexicans who are brought into the United States to work temporarily in the fields.

civil rights: the rights every person has in a free society, including freedom of speech and religion and the rights to hold a job and receive equal treatment under the law.

communist: a person who believes a government should own all or most property and should control the economy.

confiscated: seized by the government.

discrimination: unfair treatment of people based on race, religion, gender, political views, or sexual orientation.

Filipino: from the Philippines.

grassroots: based on the ordinary people in a group rather than on the group's leaders or those who give money to the group.

labor union: a group of workers that bargains with employers and lobbies for better wages and working conditions.

lobby: try to influence powerful people for or against a cause.

migrant workers: laborers who travel from place to place looking for work.

nonviolent confrontation: opposing someone without resorting to violence.

organized: formed a labor union.

picket lines: groups of people who form a line to protest the policies of an employer or organization and discourage others from being involved with that employer or organization.

posthumously: after someone has died.

social activist: someone who actively fights social injustice.

Soviet Union: a communist nation that consisted of present-day Russia and other, neighboring countries and existed from 1922 to 1991.

strike: a work stoppage by a group of workers to protest unacceptable wages or working conditions.

tangible: having an actual value that can be measured.

TO FIND OUT MORE

BOOKS

Brown, Adele Q. *Martin Luther King, Jr. (Trailblazers of the Modern World).* Milwaukee: World Almanac Library, 2003.

Collins, David R. *Farmworker's Friend: The Story of César Chávez.* Minneapolis: Lerner, 1996.

de Ruiz, Dana Catharine and Richard Larios. *La Causa: The Migrant Farmworkers' Story.* Austin: Steck-Vaughn Company, 1993.

Heinrichs, Anne. *Mahatma Gandhi (Trailblazers of the Modern World).* Milwaukee: World Almanac Library, 2001.

Perez, Frank. *Dolores Huerta.* Austin: Raintree Steck-Vaughn, 1996.

Wheeler, Jill C. *César Chávez.* Edina, Minn: ABDO Publishing Company, 2003.

INTERNET SITES

The Bracero Program
http://www.bigchalk.com/cgi-bin/WebObjects/WOPortal.woa/wa/HWCDA/file?fileid=214855&flt=CAB&tg=ARTS
Provides information on this often-exploited group of workers from other countries.

Viva César E. Chávez!
http://www.sfsu.edu/%7Ececipp/César_Chávez/Chávezhome.htm
A collection of audio clips from Chávez's speeches, photos, interviews, and news articles.

Honoring César Estrada Chávez
http://www.migente.com/Members/Home/Chávez_01/
Explains why California celebrates César E. Chávez day on March 31 of every year. Includes interviews with those people who knew Chávez.

United Farm Workers
http://www.ufw.org
Covers issues of importance to farm workers and their supporters. Provides a history of the farm workers' movement, including biographies of César Chávez, Dolores Huerta, and others.

About the Author

Jonatha A. Brown has a broad background in writing and editing, much of it as a free-lancer helping corporations develop interactive computer-based training programs. A native of Rochester, New York, Jonny holds a BA in English from St. Lawrence University in Canton, New York. She currently lives in Phoenix, Arizona, with her husband and two dogs. She is delighted to be taking a break from corporate life by working with horses and writing books for children.